DOUBLE EXPOSURE

Gillian Philip

Illustrated by **Euan Cook**

OXFORD
UNIVERSITY PRESS

Letter from the Author

I'm fascinated by the way all kinds of art and writing use the contrast between light and dark. This story was inspired by my daughter's photography project, all about nature surviving in cities.

When Martin and Sophia are partnered in a school photography competition, they have to work out how to balance not only their very different approaches to photography, but also their time and other priorities. Since they've never exactly been the best of friends, they have to do it without falling out!

I always knew I wanted to be a writer – as a child I spent all my pocket money on notebooks and all my time writing stories in them. Now I get to write stories for a living! I hope you enjoy this one.

Gillian Philip

Chapter 1
Miss Bartlett's Challenge

My heart flipped when I saw the poster.
It's a funny thing. When my heart does that, I imagine I hear a camera shutter. You know, that whispery rattle-and-click that even smartphones make. They put that noise in phones even though there's no reason for it, because people expect it when they take a photo. It's my favourite sound in the world.

Anyway, the posters must have gone up overnight. They were in every corridor, but the first one I saw was right in the middle of the noticeboard by reception, half-covering the older notices about the school concert, and the sponsored walk, and the permanent sign that says BREAKNESS PRIMARY SCHOOL MISSION STATEMENT!

This is what the new poster said:

CALLING ALL PHOTOGRAPHERS!
Miss Bartlett's Art Club announces The Breakness Primary School Photo Competition!

My school only ever seemed to run competitions for Maths, or writing stories, or designing road safety posters, and I wasn't any good at any of those.

But I was very good at taking photographs.

It was almost too good to be true. I wasn't quite sure what I'd do with *two* Pocket Digital Cameras, but I'd work that out later, because finally there was something I could win. I hadn't even read to the bottom of the poster, but I already knew I had to win first prize. I could almost see my photo already, printed in the local paper. I was so excited I actually had trouble breathing for a moment.

Then I read down to the end of the poster.

Can you work as a team?
Pick a partner and get creative!
All entries must be from teams of two.

So I was right: it *was* too good to be true. That explained why there were two of every prize.

My head reeled at the unfairness of it. How could a team photograph anything? And even if that was possible, where was I supposed to find a teammate?

The only people in the Art Club I was friendly with were Ace and Daniel, and since they teamed up with each other for everything, neither of them was going to be an option. The rest of the club were girls who always wanted to pair up with their best buddies. Miss Bartlett, who ran the club, was friendly, but that doesn't count as a friend. You certainly don't go around asking teachers to be your competition-buddy. Apart from a few pictures on their parents' phones, none of my other mates were at all interested in photography. I was on my own.

I was still staring in horrified disbelief at the bit about being in a team of two when I heard someone yell my name. 'Marty! Hey, Marty!'

I groaned, but very quietly so she wouldn't hear me. I hated being called Marty, especially by Alisha and her mates. But, also, because it was Alisha and her mates, I didn't dare to complain.

I turned round, feeling my face redden. 'Hi, Alisha. Hi, Maryam. Hi, Daisy.'

'You seen it? The competition thing?' Alisha wasn't smiling but there was the usual hint of mockery in her eyes. She seemed to spend her life making fun of other people, and she found me an easy target – maybe because she knew how much I hated it. 'That'll be right up your street,' she went on when I didn't reply. 'You're such a camera nerd.'

I muttered something even I couldn't quite make out. Then I managed to say, 'Uh-huh.'

'Go for it, Marty!' Daisy flicked back her hair, grinning. 'Fame at last!'

Maryam was a bit more sullen; she always was. 'Never see the point of cameras,' she sniffed. 'My dad says you can do anything on a phone.'

'Don't let Sophia hear you say that,' said Alisha, twisting one of her dark curls. 'You know what she's like about that fancy camera that used to be her mum's.' Then her eyes lit up with mischief. Not the nice kind, either. 'Hey, Marty! Maybe you could pair up with Sophia!'

'As if,' snorted Daisy. 'Can you imagine?'

They were all giggling now, and I felt as if my jumper didn't fit me any more. It might have been throttling me; I could feel my face going redder by the second. I mumbled something else and edged away, then started walking fast down the corridor.

Not fast enough. Alisha and her pals weren't following me, but another familiar voice rang in my ears. 'Martin. Martin!'

I couldn't pretend I hadn't heard, so I turned.

Miss Bartlett hurried towards me. 'I hope you're coming to the club after school tomorrow.'

I nodded, staring at my shoes. 'Yes, Miss Bartlett.'

'And you're going to enter the competition, right? Did you see my poster?' Her voice brimmed with excitement.

'Umm,' I said. 'I'm not sure I can get a partner.'

'Oh! Oh!' She gave me a brilliant smile. 'No, this is perfect! Guess what?'

'What?' I had a horrible feeling then. I almost knew what she was going to say and yet I couldn't believe it until she did.

'Sophia Sanders hasn't got a partner either! You two can team up!'

My heart plummeted. 'I don't think – I mean, I'm not sure how you can do it as a team anyway and – '

'I'm going to explain about the teams at Art Club tomorrow. Oh, this is great, Martin.' She wasn't even listening to me, and she certainly wasn't looking at my face. If she'd seen my expression, she'd have known what a ridiculous idea this was. 'I'll go and tell Sophia. There's the bell – you'd better get to class. See you later!'

I was caught up in the tide of people pouring in from the playground, so I couldn't even stand still for a second and think. Instead I let the others jostle me into the classroom, while I wondered desperately how I could get out of this.

I should have seen it coming. Of course Sophia wouldn't have a partner.

It wasn't that I didn't want to work with Sophia (if I had to work with anybody). But I knew perfectly well what Sophia would think of the idea.

Even though she went to Art Club, I don't think she'd ever spoken to me. She didn't speak to many people at all. Sophia Sanders was probably the coolest kid in Breakness Primary, although she didn't much like mixing with other people. Maybe it was because of that. Or maybe she was just a bit full of herself: apparently her mother used to be a famous journalist or something.

Anyway, nobody spoke to Sophia unless it was clear she wanted to be spoken to. Sometimes she hung out with Alisha and her friends, but mostly Sophia just enjoyed her own company and looked scornful. Everybody else was in awe of her.

So I was surprised when the bell rang at the end of the day and she was waiting for me outside the school gate. I was less surprised that she had a face like thunder.

She didn't even say hello. 'Have you heard this rubbish? Have you?'

I swallowed. It wasn't just the way she spoke; Sophia even looked intimidating. Her dark eyes gave off a death stare.

'You mean about the photo competition?' I asked.

Sophia nodded sharply. 'Miss Bartlett says we have to work together.'

I'd known she was going to be annoyed, but I was still a bit hurt. 'It's not that bad, is it? Being in a team with me?'

She sighed and rolled her eyes. 'Look, Martin, it's nothing personal. I just don't see how teams work. It's a ridiculous idea.'

'I know,' I admitted. 'Miss Bartlett says she's going to explain it at Art Club. So I guess we'll hear then, but it sounds like we have to do it. We can't enter otherwise.'

'Yeah.' Sophia scowled. 'And I am going to enter.'

'You mean we are,' I pointed out. 'Since we don't have a choice.'

'Yes, Martin, yes, whatever.' She gave a dramatic sigh. 'Everybody else has got a partner already. I checked. And your photos aren't bad, I guess. So I suppose we'll work something out.'

She was just as prickly as I'd imagined, then. I hesitated to ask, but I did: 'So can I see some of your photos, then? And you can look at mine.'

'Not at my place,' she said quickly. 'And not on a phone – you can't really see them properly. The school computers would be better.'

'All right.' I chewed my lip. 'Can you bring yours on a memory stick tomorrow? I'll bring mine and we can talk at the club.'

'Fine.'

Sophia hadn't said hello, and she didn't say goodbye either. She just turned and stalked off towards the bus stop, her school bag bouncing against her back.

Chapter 2
Owls and Alleyways

'Now,' said Miss Bartlett, 'I know you've all been asking about the team part of the competition.'

Everyone in the Art room looked at each other. Nobody had a clue how teams were supposed to work, but nobody wanted to say it.

Except for Ace, of course, who had a Class Clown reputation to live up to. 'You both hold the camera and race to see who clicks first.'

Miss Bartlett gave him the usual slightly strained laugh. 'No, Ace. What I want you to do is make a collage. Pick a theme, and take some photos that illustrate it. Arrange them together on a big display. That way, we get to see how two people approach the same subject. How their ideas work together!'

I caught the look Sophia shot me. It was not the look of someone who was going to enjoy sharing artistic opinions with me.

'And the other thing I want you to do,' Miss Bartlett went on, 'is caption each other's photos on the collage.'

This time, the glance Sophia gave me was one of pure horror.

Miss Bartlett clapped her hands briskly together. 'I think this will make it much more interesting than just submitting single photos. I'm really looking forward to seeing everyone's work!'

Ace and Daniel already had their heads together, murmuring and giggling. I just knew they were going to come up with wildly silly captions that would make everyone laugh. I wished I was teamed up with one of them.

Sophia got up and walked over to me. Again, there was no introductory hello. 'I suppose we'd better start coming up with ideas, then.'

'I suppose. Did you bring your memory stick?' I asked her.

'Yeah. How unfair is this?' She walked at my side to one of the class computers. 'I'm sure your photos are great but I don't think yours are going to work with mine.'

'You never know,' I mumbled, a bit offended. 'We'd better give it a shot anyway.'

I typed the wrong password twice before I managed to log on. I suppose I must have been nervous, even though I told myself I wasn't. I knew my photos were good and there was no reason Sophia shouldn't like them, so I had no excuse for shaky fingers. Maybe it was just that she was leaning on the chair back behind me, glaring over my shoulder at the screen. That was enough to put anybody on edge.

I found I was holding my breath as the pictures loaded and I scrolled through them. Sophia was silent for a very long time. I hoped it was because she was speechless with admiration. Anybody can photograph ducks if you carry some bread scraps around, but it had taken me ages to get the sparrowhawk right, even though it hunted around our garden. And, as for the owl, Mum had taken me down to the public hide in the park at dusk and we'd sat there with a flask and sandwiches for what felt like hours.

It had been worth it, though. I'd got a really good shot of the owl in flight, with Mum's posh and complicated camera, just as the last light was fading on the boating lake. I'd saved that picture for last, so I sat back and let Sophia look at it for a while.

'Humph,' she said at last. 'Well, it's pretty, I suppose.'

I turned my head and gaped at her. I couldn't help it. *'Pretty?'*

'I mean, it is. I like it. It's nice to look at.'

'So what's wrong with it?'

'Well, it's just an owl. Flying.'

I never thought I'd dare to snap at Sophia Sanders. 'It took me ages to get that! It was really hard!'

'Yeah, I'm sure.' She tilted her head to one side and frowned. I was speechless.

'But it doesn't say much,' she went on, 'except "Here's an owl".'

'All right,' I snapped, then lowered my voice as Miss Bartlett gave us a concerned look. 'Let's see what your pictures are *saying*.'

I stood up, scraping back the chair a little violently. Sophia sat down and plugged in her memory card. I noticed the back of her neck going red as she opened up the picture file. She fiddled with her choppy black hair.

So she wasn't all that confident, then.

I leaned over to peer at her photos as she clicked. I was already wondering what on earth had made Miss Bartlett think we'd make a good team.

'What's that?' I asked. 'Cobbles?'

Sophia made a face; I could see it reflected in the screen. 'It's the alley behind the amusement arcade. You know, at the beachfront.'

'It's just the ground.' I wrinkled my nose. 'There's rubbish everywhere. Look, there's a squashed can, crisp packets ... '

'That's the point.' Sophia gave a loud, irritated sigh. 'It's all about gritty reality, see. Mean Streets, my mum says. And my mum's a real photographer, a professional.' She licked her lips and muttered, 'Was, anyway.'

I peered closer. There was nothing else in the black-and-white picture, just those dirty cobbles. Maybe they made an interesting pattern? But not that interesting.

'It's a bit depressing,' I said.

'Oh, is that what you're going to put as the caption?' She swung her head round, bristling. '"It's a bit depressing"?'

'Well, what are you going to put on mine?' I snapped. '"Here's an owl"? My mum's a photographer too, you know.' It was true. I didn't want to add Mum was only an amateur birdwatcher. After all, she'd had her bird photos printed in actual magazines. That was kind of like being a professional.

'Look, I think your photos are nice.' Sophia leaned back and folded her arms. 'I mean they're good. But I like to do real life. Stuff that means something. Ugly stuff too.'

'What's wrong with a picture people want to look at?' I clicked on to another of her photos. 'Who wants to look at an earwig?'

'Earwigs are interesting! Unlike ducks. Ducks are just fat birds that have it easy. My mum was a war photographer, and you don't have to like looking at her pictures but they're really, really *important*.'

We glared at each other for a long moment. I was actually quite impressed that Sophia's mum had been a war photographer, but that didn't make a snap of old cobbles *important* and *interesting*.

Somebody had to break the silence. 'We'd better have a go at finding something to photograph.'

'Fine.' Sophia shrugged. 'Tomorrow's Saturday. Why don't we meet up at the beach? There'll be birds there.'

She was probably planning to photograph the overflowing bins outside the ice cream shop, I thought, but it was a start. Maybe I could get her interested in some seashells or something.

'OK. We could meet up at the car park? I'll get my dad to give me a lift down.'

'Make it the bus shelter. That's not far from my house – I'm in Broxden Street. It's quicker for me to walk there.'

'OK.' I didn't realize she'd have to walk – or be allowed to. Her mother must be easy-going. 'After lunch?'

Sophia nodded and opened her mouth to speak, but just at that moment, Miss Bartlett came bustling over.

'You two have been exchanging lots of ideas, I noticed! I'm so glad.' Miss Bartlett glanced doubtfully at the ferocious-looking earwig that filled the computer screen. Then she smiled, brightly. 'You're going to come up with some great work between you!'

Miss Bartlett didn't see Sophia roll her eyes. But I did. I stifled a sigh. We weren't going to win a thing in this competition, were we?

There seemed to be just the one question:

How spectacularly were we going to lose?

Chapter 3
Artistic Differences

The beach was just as enticing as it always was. In other words, heavy unbroken cloud loomed from horizon to horizon and a cold breeze sliced across the seafront, sending a tattered plastic bag swooping and blustering into the wall of the bus shelter.

'Looks freezing,' said my dad with a dramatic shiver. 'You have fun. I'll be in the cafe over there, with a hot coffee and the newspaper.'

As he hurried across the road I was tempted to ask if I could join him and drink hot chocolate instead of hanging around a windswept beach. Just then, though, I saw Sophia hurrying towards me along the promenade, hunched against the wind.

Her eyes brightened as she came nearer, but I didn't think for a minute she was pleased to see me. I was right. She pulled an elaborate, professional-looking camera out of its bag, brought it to her eye, and paused to fiddle with the long lens. Then she rapid-fire clicked at the plastic bag that was now splattered against the dirty glass of the bus shelter.

'It's a bag,' I said with strained patience. 'From the supermarket.'

Sophia shot me a scornful look. 'It's a symbol, that's what it is.'

Clearly we had both silently decided that we were never going to bother with 'Hello'.

'Symbol of what?' I asked. 'The Breakness litter problem?'

'Futility,' she snapped.

'I don't even know what that is.' I shrugged.

She flushed a little, and I wondered if she wasn't totally sure either. 'It means it's bleak. It's desolate. It hasn't got any point. Like this town.'

I bristled. Breakness wasn't the Costa del Heatwave, but I quite liked living here. In June it could be downright balmy. For a day or two, midweek. 'You don't have to be so negative,' I told her.

'And you don't have to be Mister Sunshine all the time.' Peering at her camera, she twisted off the lens, stowed it in the bag and snapped on an even longer one.

That camera of hers was really very impressive. My fingers itched for a go at it. I decided I should try being nice.

'So what do you want to do first?' I asked. 'We could go down to the shore.'

'I suppose.' She frowned in concentration. 'I guess you'd be interested in those seagulls.'

'They're just called gulls,' I said. I couldn't help myself, though I knew it was a mistake.

Sophia glowered at me for a moment. Then she spun on her heel and marched off towards the chipped concrete steps that led down to the beach.

I rolled my eyes, annoyed at myself for saying the wrong thing. *Nice one, Martin.*

I jogged to catch up with Sophia. The gulls were fighting over the remains of a bag of chips, so I should have known that would catch her interest. She crouched a little way from them and brought her camera to her face. The gulls took no notice of either of us; they just went on flapping and screeching and stabbing with their yellow beaks at grimy, sodden chips.

We walked closer to them across the wet sand. Now and again Sophia would pause cautiously and take a few more shots. But by the time the birds finally bothered with us, enough to swivel their heads and glare and take off in a flurry of white wings, we could almost have reached out and touched them.

'Let me see, then,' I said, curious.

A little hesitantly, Sophia held out the camera so I could look at the screen on the back. Needless to say, there wasn't much gull to be seen in her pictures. A darting beak or an occasional dangling webbed foot made its way into the frame, but mostly she'd focused on the limp chip bag, tumbling in the edge of the waves.

'Interesting,' was all I could say.

'Exactly,' she told me, triumphantly.

I swung my own camera at my side, unsure how to begin explaining. 'Don't you think they're kind of beautiful, though?' I asked.

'What, the seagulls?' she said loudly, as if she was trying to goad me by using the wrong word.

'Yeah.'

'They're savages.' She shrugged. 'I saw them nick an ice cream off a little old lady last week.'

'Well, I know,' I admitted. 'I mean they can be brutes, but they're still beautiful.'

Sophia gave me a funny look, wrinkling her nose. 'Whatever you say, Martin.'

'Look.' I unsnapped my lens cap and scanned the sky. I found one of the gulls, its belly and wings shining bright white against the dirty clouds. Zooming in, I snapped a few pictures, then showed the screen to Sophia. 'See? Beautiful.'

She jabbed a finger at the display. 'Yes,' she agreed, 'but the clouds are more interesting. Look at the colour of that one. Filthy grey. Heavy and threatening, like it's going to fall right on us.'

I gave an impatient sigh. This was not going to work. The shoreline certainly was bleak, just as Sophia seemed to like it; to me the gulls were the only interesting thing around. A woman walked her dog, briskly, as if she wanted nothing more than to get back to her car. Two teenagers sat on the sea wall sharing a single bag of chips; maybe the gulls had stolen the second one. There was a lone guy in a wetsuit, gripping a surfboard and staring at the waves without much enthusiasm. Up on the promenade, two mothers shoved pushchairs against the wind.

As I watched them, the plastic bag from the bus shelter bounced and flapped down the beach, as if it were following us. It was definitely the same one. For a moment it ballooned and floated like a jellyfish, and I saw Sophia snatch up her camera again and focus on it.

'Why don't you photograph something that looks good?' I exclaimed crossly. 'How are we going to win this if you only take rubbish?'

'It's not rubbish!' She turned on me, her eyes flashing. 'And even if it is, the pictures aren't!'

'What's the point?' I wasn't backing down. 'Who wants to look at a plastic bag?'

'You know what your trouble is?' Sophia smacked the cap on so hard I thought she was going to break the lens. 'You think life's all pretty birds and flowers.'

'Flowers?' I gasped, offended. 'Flowers have got nothing to do—'

'Sometimes the world is a bit grim, you know!'

she ranted, ignoring me. 'There are wars – and famine and misery – and dirty old shopping bags! And that all needs photographing too!'

'Maybe it does, but you won't find anyone who wants to look at it.'

'You're so – ' Sophia licked her lips as if she couldn't think of a bad enough word for me. 'So *shallow*!'

I'd had enough. The dog-walking woman had stopped to stare at us despite the cold, and the teenagers on the sea wall were sniggering, but I didn't care. I yelled, 'Well, you can forget about the competition! We haven't got a chance.'

'Too right we haven't.' Sophia's face was bright red with fury. 'Go and take a selfie with a sparrow or something. I'm out of here.'

I watched her storm off, back up towards the promenade. The man in the wetsuit was staring too, but I didn't care. And I was far too furious to call Sophia back.

This was the only competition I'd ever had a chance of winning.

And she'd ruined everything.

Chapter 4
Looking for Sophia

The trouble was, I really did care about winning Miss Bartlett's infuriating competition. I felt defiant and completely in the right, but by the time I'd taken about forty photos of the undersides of gulls, my fingers were freezing and I'd calmed down enough to be miserable instead of angry.

The plastic bag had bounced and blown further down the beach, so I chased it and picked it up between my fingertips. With a sense of grim satisfaction I shoved it into a bin and trudged down to the pedestrian crossing.

Dad waved through the cafe window, and the little bell tinkled as I pushed open the door. Oh, it

was lovely and warm in there. It didn't make me feel much better, though.

'How did it go?' he asked, pushing back his chair. 'I take it you need a hot chocolate.'

'Yeah,' I nodded. 'Please.'

'It's a deal. If you show me your photos after. I can't wait to see what you've come up with!'

While Dad waited at the counter, I flicked through the pictures I'd taken. They didn't cheer me up as much as I'd thought they would. They were all a bit too similar, to be honest. They were good, even if I said so myself, but one gull did look a lot like the next gull.

Except for that one.

I cupped a hand round the display to shade it and peered into the screen, frowning.

It wasn't a gull after all, it was the plastic bag. Just like the birds, it glowed white against the dark and gloomy clouds. The gulls soared around it as if it were one of the flock. It looked almost cheerful, flapping there in the sky.

I was starting to get an idea.

* * *

'This is a good idea, Martin,' said Dad, stopping the car at the end of Broxden Street. 'I know you'll want to make up with Sophia. And I thought those photos were great!'

Dad always thought my photos were great, so that didn't mean much. I made a face. 'I don't think it's going to be easy,' I mumbled.

'Nothing in life is easy,' he told me briskly, clapping me on the shoulder as I took off my seatbelt. (It was one of his favourite sayings, and I'd seen it coming, so I didn't even reply.) 'I'll be back at, let's see ... five o'clock?'

'Four,' I said quickly, and got out of the car.

At least here the houses gave a bit of shelter, and you didn't get the sea wind slicing through your skin, but it still wasn't what you'd call warm. As Dad drove off I stood there hopping from foot to foot, feeling a bit daft, because I realized I had no idea which house was Sophia's. Broxden Street wasn't enormous, but nor was it so short that I could just go knocking on doors till I found her.

I sighed and took a picture of a one-legged pigeon.

'Well, look who it is!' A familiar voice made me look up. Already my heart was sinking. 'Hey, Marty!'

'Hey, Alisha,' I mumbled.

She, Daisy and Maryam were fooling around on skateboards outside one of the houses. They stopped when they saw me and Alisha snatched up her board and came towards me, eyes bright with mischief and mockery. 'Did you finally find a partner?'

'Um,' I said, and licked my lips nervously as they surrounded me. 'Um. I'm … It's me and Sophia. We're a team.'

Alisha's jaw dropped. 'You are kidding me!'

'Seriously?' Daisy boggled at me.

'No way,' said Maryam. 'How did *that* happen?'

'I can't believe Sophia agreed to that,' laughed Alisha.

'She didn't,' I snapped, suddenly annoyed. 'And neither did I! Miss Bartlett made us.'

'Ohhh.' Alisha's eyes widened. 'That explains it, then. Poor old Sophia.'

'Poor old me,' I retorted. I wasn't sure where I was getting the nerve, but suddenly I was really tired of Alisha's teasing. I was fed up with her making fun of my photography. I was fed up with being the weird camera nerd, and I was fed up with Sophia's surly attitude, and I really, really wanted to win that competition. I glared right into Alisha's eyes. 'Sophia's really bad-tempered about it, and she's not helping, and it's not like it's my fault.'

Alisha blinked, as if she couldn't quite decide how to react. Then she laughed, but for once, not in a nasty way. 'Oh, I get that.' She exchanged glances with Daisy and Maryam. 'It's not like Sophia's easy, right?'

They giggled.

'She's so difficult,' said Daisy, rolling her eyes.

Alisha gave her a scowl and her tone became severe. 'She's got an excuse though.'

Daisy grunted and looked sheepish. 'Sure.'

'You're kind of wasting your time, Marty,' Alisha told me. 'Sophia can't really be bothered with other people.'

'She's friends with you,' I pointed out.

'Well, kind of.' Alisha wrinkled her nose. 'We live on the same street and I've known her since nursery. Look, she's cool, but she really just puts up with us.'

'She's super spiky,' said Daisy, tossing her hair. 'She's not going to go out of her way to be friends with *you*.'

Alisha sighed. 'Why are you bothering, Marty?'

'It's just ... ' I took a breath. 'It's just that I've got an idea. For working together.'

Alisha narrowed her eyes. 'She won't want your advice, you know.'

'I thought we could, you know ... help each other,' I insisted.

Alisha threw an arm round my shoulder, making me jump. 'You'd better not say that to her. You know what Sophia's trouble is? She doesn't want help. Not from anybody.'

'It's not – it's not me helping her,' I protested. 'I just want us to work together. At least, I want to ask her. If she wants to. You know.'

Alisha was silent for a long moment, eyeing me thoughtfully. 'Tell you what,' she said at last. 'Sophia's not looking for friends, and she's not a team player, exactly, but she's not that scary when you get to know her.' She shrugged. 'And I know she'll want to win that boring competition too.'

'It's not boring.' Suddenly I felt almost bold. 'And she'd say the same. But we're not even going to enter it if I can't talk to her, and I'm trying to find her but I don't know where she lives.'

Alisha raised her eyebrows at Daisy and Maryam.

Maryam shrugged. 'We could tell him which house it is.'

'Hmm. OK.' Alisha nodded and let go of my shoulders. 'If you promise to be nice to our friend, I think we can help.'

Chapter 5
Light and Dark

I didn't really think it was that way round – me making an effort to be nice to Sophia – but once I'd agreed, Alisha was as good as her word. That was how I found myself almost tiptoeing down Sophia's street, not nearly as brave now that I knew where I was going. The houses further along the street were quite big, set back from the road with their own front gardens, and they made the idea of ringing Sophia's doorbell even more nerve-racking.

I guessed which one was hers before I even saw the number. All the gardens were neat and trimmed – some were completely paved for cars – except for that one. The shrubs were straggly, and the yellowed square of lawn didn't look as if it had been cut in ages. I don't know why I immediately thought of Sophia, but it turned out I was right.

I creaked the gate open and shuffled up the path, my heart hammering. By the time I walked up the ramp to the door I thought I might just turn around and walk away. The competition wasn't everything.

Except it was. And if I could face terrifying, scornful Alisha, I could ring this bell.

I gritted my teeth and rang it.

It seemed to take Sophia forever to answer it – long enough for me to change my mind several times about staying put. I was beginning to wonder if she was even at home, when the door was suddenly flung open.

Sophia stood glaring at me, her expression half irritation and half surprise. The surprise won.

'What are you doing here?' she asked.

'Hello,' I said. I thought I should really start saying that.

'Hello, Martin.' She looked even more startled, but that was definitely almost a smile.

'I don't think we should give up on this competition,' I blurted. 'Not yet, anyway.'

She glanced past me, up and down the street, then back over her shoulder. She bit her lip.

'Maybe,' she said warily. 'This isn't a good time, though.'

'It's got to be,' I said firmly. 'We haven't *got* much time.'

Sophia stared at me for a moment, then heaved a resigned sigh. 'All right. Come in, then. But you'll have to be quiet.'

She stood back, beckoning me inside. The hallway was dim as I crept in, and it took a moment for my eyes to adjust. When they did, I saw that there were framed photos everywhere, rows of them, from halfway up the walls nearly to the ceiling.

'Come through to the kitchen,' she hissed, but I couldn't. I was too busy looking at the pictures. The places all looked exotic and faraway: blue skies and sandy pitted roads, crumbling buildings, glaring light. Some were all bright blotches of colour, others coated in a muddy yellow-brown dust. It was the people who stood out, though. Some of them stared at the camera in bleak resignation; others looked fiercely down the camera lens. There were pictures of soldiers, and children, and exhausted barefooted men and women.

'Wow,' I breathed. 'These are really powerful.'

'Come on,' Sophia whispered, more loudly. She beckoned me towards a door at the end of the hall.

'Sophia, who's that?' a new voice called out.

Sophia squeezed her eyes shut. 'See? I told you to be quiet!' she hissed angrily. 'It's OK, Mum,' she called. 'Just a friend.'

'Well, why can't I meet him?' called the voice again, cheerfully.

For a moment Sophia hesitated, then she shrugged. 'Fine,' she muttered. 'This way, but don't tire her out!'

She opened another door and almost shoved me into a big living room.

The light was brighter in here. A woman watched me with very keen eyes from an armchair. She had an angular, serious sort of face, streaky hair drawn back in a rough ponytail and, even though she was sitting down, she gave the impression of being very tall. There was something stiff and unnatural about the way she sat, angled sideways into the corner of the chair. If her eyes hadn't been twinkling, she'd have been almost as intimidating as Sophia.

'This is Martin,' said Sophia. 'Martin, this is
my mum.'

'Hello, Martin. Excuse me if I don't get up,'
she smiled.

'That's OK,' I mumbled, embarrassed. I suddenly
noticed the wheelchair parked behind her seat, and
I remembered the ramp at the door and blushed
a little. 'Your photos are amazing, Mrs Sanders,'
I blurted.

There were more of them in this room – not as many as in the hall, but still plenty, some of them in stand-up frames on tables.

'Thank you.' Unhooking one of those handy-grabbers from the arm of her chair, she used it to pick up one of the photos. She almost dropped it, but shut the jaws of the grabber in the nick of time. She stretched the photo out to me awkwardly and I took it, feeling a little hesitant. I wondered what she was about to show me.

But for once the photo showed a group of people grinning, looking happy, their arms around one another, and Sophia's mum was one of them. 'That's me and my friends. Are you the photographer I've heard about, Martin?'

I nodded, feeling myself go red again. 'Not a proper one. It's just a hobby.'

'That makes you a proper one.' Mrs Sanders smiled again. She had a very friendly smile.

'Most of these are probably a bit depressing for Martin,' said Sophia with an edge of scorn. 'He doesn't like – y'know, gritty stuff.'

I was going to die of embarrassment any minute. 'I do!' I protested.

'Oh, I suppose it's a bit odd to have them all on display.' Sophia's mum grinned. 'They're not exactly, um ... cheerful. But I like to see them. They remind me of my job, when I had it. And how much I valued it. But they're not beautiful, I'm afraid.'

'No!' I was surprised how strongly I felt about it, but it was true. 'They are beautiful. Well, I think so.'

'That's funny coming from you.' Sophia leaned on a chair back, giving me a sarcastic look. 'You don't like my photos, and they're not half as dark as some of these.'

'That's not true, really ... I ... ' I swallowed hard. 'Look, that's what I wanted to talk to you about.'

Sophia's mum wasn't smiling at me any more; she was looking at me very keenly. 'Well, you two obviously do need to talk,' she said. 'Why don't you go up to my old study, Sophia? You can take my laptop if you like, so you can look at your photos.'

'Are you sure?' Sophia bit her lip. 'Not about the laptop. I mean, will you be OK? You're not hungry or anything?'

Her mum gave a wry laugh. 'Darling, I'm OK for hours while you're at school. Off you go, and give me some peace.'

'OK, Mum, if you're sure.' Sophia grabbed my arm and almost bundled me out of the living room.

'Your mum seems nice,' I said as I followed her up the steep stairs.

'Of course she is,' said Sophia without turning round. 'She's not always in that good a mood. But she's nice.'

'What's, er ... '

'Wrong with her? She's got MS,' Sophia told me curtly as she darted into a room and emerged clutching a laptop. 'That's all. Now, come in here and we'll look at the pictures.' She flung open a door, revealing a small room that was thickly lined with books and file boxes. There was a small desk at the window, thinly covered in dust.

'Is that why you're off school a lot? Have you got to look after her?' I didn't know quite where I was finding the nerve, but I was burning with curiosity. 'Is it just you?'

'Yes. Yes. And sort of.' Sophia set the laptop

down on the desk and plugged in her memory stick. 'Now be quiet and tell me what you're thinking.'

I can't do both of those at the same time, I thought resentfully, but I managed not to say it. 'It's just, I had an idea. For how we can make this project work.'

'I'm not making pretty collages of birds and flowers, if that's what you think.' Defiantly she clicked on the shot of the plastic bag smeared across the bus shelter glass. 'Why did you lie to my mum? You don't like those kinds of pictures.'

'I was not lying!' I snapped.

'Oh yeah? Did you really, really love the one of the village that had been destroyed?'

I shuddered. 'Course not. Well – not that way. I didn't love it. But there was something about it. Something that made you want to look at it. Like you couldn't take your eyes off it.'

'Oh, you make no sense,' she said, exasperated.

'I know, but I'm trying. Look.' I leaned across her shoulder to show her the display screen on my camera. 'I think you're right. My pictures don't say anything. They're just kind of pretty and bland. I know what you mean, now.'

'OK.' She sounded a bit mollified. 'A seagull's just a seagull, right?'

'Right.' I swallowed my pride. 'But – a plastic bag is – well, just a plastic bag.'

She twisted her head to glare at me. 'But it's real life. Don't you get that? Real life isn't pretty for a lot of people. It's sad and hard and miserable!'

'Don't get mad at me.' I took a breath, reminding myself that I wanted to make this team work. I counted to five. 'Look, I took this by accident.' I clicked through to the photo of the flying bag against the clouds.

'That's beautiful,' she said, and then chewed hard on her lip as if she instantly regretted saying it.

I tried to keep my mouth shut too. Sophia was still staring at the picture. Kind of like she couldn't take her eyes off it.

At last she shoved her chair back from the desk. 'But that's just you making it pretty again. That's not the point. It's not meant to be pretty. I don't want to take photos like yours!'

'I made you look, though. I made you look at it.' Desperately I tried to think how I could explain it;

I could hardly explain it to myself. 'I don't want you to take pictures like mine, that's the thing. I think your ideas are great. Much more interesting than mine.'

She tilted her head at me, looking suspicious. 'So I'll pick the ideas, then?'

'Yes!'

'You're not trying to tell me how to do this?'

'No!'

'OK.' She narrowed her eyes. 'Because I do *not* like being told how to do stuff.'

Yeah, I think I've got that. 'But, um … can we mix it up with my kind of photos? Make people want to look. 'Cause, you know, if you make them look, they'll see it better. They'll get what you're saying.'

Sophia opened her mouth as if she was going to argue, then shut it again. She leaned in to peer at my camera, then plugged it into the laptop and brought up a bigger version of the plastic-bag-gull.

'It really does look like it's flying,' she mused. She flicked the screen with a fingernail. 'The way that dirty old bag's lit up, like the birds. It's like it's one of them.'

'Or not really.' I fidgeted with the collar of my jumper. 'But like it's a plastic bag ... '

' ... trying to be a seagull,' she finished. She was grinning.

'It's doing its best,' I added. Suddenly it seemed quite funny, but sad at the same time.

'It's never going to be a seagull, but it's going to have a go.' Sophia was actually laughing now. 'I get it. It's still just an old plastic bag but it can be beautiful. It can be something else. It's a horrible bit of litter but you can look at it another way.'

'See it like it sees itself!' I grinned. Suddenly I remembered shoving it in the bin, and I felt a tiny twinge of guilt, as if I'd crushed its dreams. 'You don't think we're, um ... making too much fun of it?'

Sophia turned and gazed at me solemnly. 'I don't think we need to worry about hurting its feelings,' she told me. 'It's a plastic bag.'

I giggled. I couldn't help it. 'Remember a couple of weeks ago when Miss Bartlett was explaining about black-and-white photography?'

'When she was banging on and on about it, you mean? Reminded me of my mum. Yeah, go on.'

'It was all about the contrast, she said. Between the light and the dark, when that's all you've got to, kind of, play with. Showing up the brightness by making the dark bits really dark. And the other way round. The way the plastic bag's dirty and an eyesore but it can look beautiful in the right situation.' One of these days I was going to stop blushing and fumbling my words. 'Sort of like that. You know.'

Sophia wasn't laughing at me; she'd gone serious again. 'Did you notice that photo on the mantelpiece in the living room? The one with the woman cooking.'

I remembered it, even though I'd been in awe of Sophia's mum. 'She's standing in the rubble and she's got a little gas stove and she's frying something.'

'That's the one. Her house has been badly damaged, but she's getting on with making some food. It's awful, she's lost her home, but I can see beauty in that picture. She's got fiery eyes. Like she's going to cook this dinner and she doesn't care who tries to stop her. Did you notice how her husband's standing there holding a spatula, looking at her like she's the only person on the planet? And it's not because she's beautiful, because she's covered in dust but—'

'But she is kind of beautiful,' I said.

'You see? That's why I love that picture. I can never stop looking at it.' She gave me a rather dark look. 'Oh, ha ha. I see what you did there.'

'I didn't do it, you did.' I grinned.

'My mum's brilliant, isn't she?' said Sophia.

'Well, your photos are pretty good too,' I said rashly. I nodded at the laptop screen. 'I'd never have thought of taking a picture of a plastic bag. That one was an accident.'

'Yeah, you're not so bad yourself.' Sophia tapped the screen again. 'I do think some of your photos are lovely, actually.'

'So ... ' I bit my lip. 'So you think we can do this, then? The competition.'

'Course we can.' Sophia stood up, kicking back the chair. 'In fact, we're going to win it.'

Chapter 5
Bugs Are Beautiful Too

'I can't be out long,' Sophia told me. It was the next day – a brighter one, with clouds scudding across the sun – and my dad had driven me down to Sophia's. We emerged blinking from her garage into the alley behind her house. 'I've got to make Mum's tea.'

I didn't see how she could be so confident of winning the competition if she couldn't spend any time on it. 'Do you really have to?'

She went stock-still and glared at me. 'She's got to eat!'

'No! I mean, are you really the only person who looks after her? Sorry!'

'I am at the moment. The carer doesn't come in again till Monday.'

I picked at a plant growing out of the wall. 'Oh, OK. That seems rough.'

'Why would it be rough? She's my mum! Honestly, people like you have got it so easy, Martin.'

I thought for a moment – a really fleeting moment – of objecting. I mean, my life wasn't all moonbeams and unicorns. There was the time my nan got sick enough to go to hospital for a whole week. And the time Mum confiscated my camera and yelled at me for not doing my homework, and the time Dad seethed for a week because the teacher called him in for a word. (Come to think of it, that was the same time, and it was about the same thing.) But ... maybe it hadn't been that bad, compared to having to look after your sick mum. Most of my problems did seem pretty minor by comparison. I'd never had to cook a meal in my life, let alone nurse somebody.

'I'm really sorry—'

'You don't need to be sorry!' Sophia snapped. 'It's not a problem!'

I was beginning to realize that Sophia was a very confusing person.

'Hey, move your hand,' she said suddenly. 'There. Pull out that weed.'

I was pretty sure my mum would not approve of pulling wild plants out of walls, even if they were weeds. But I loosened its roots a bit and wiggled it. A woodlouse curled up and squirmed in a panic as the light hit it.

'Aha!' Sophia rapidly focused her lens on it and began to click away. I was just rolling my eyes when I remembered saying that she could choose the subjects. I took a breath and counted to ten.

'Wait,' I said suddenly. 'The sun's coming out.'

She shot me an impatient look, but she paused and glanced up. A patch of blue had appeared between the clouds, and a golden light struck the wall. Sophia took a few extra shots as two more woodlice wriggled out of the roots and scuttled into cracks.

'Here, let me see.' I took the camera from her and squinted into the display screen as she watched me expectantly.

It was hard to see properly, but I got the idea.

It was a really clear close-up. The woodlice were gilded like tiny armoured horses. They and the few bits of soil that clung to the roots were in clear focus; the background was a blur of gold and purple, made up of sun-sparkles from the granite and the tiny flowers of the weed.

'Uh,' I said. 'That's lovely.'

She grinned at me.

I tucked the plant's roots back into the wall as best I could; it was tiny and pretty, but I was sure it was tough enough to survive. The woodlice had vanished again, hidden in the cool darkness between the granite blocks.

'See?' she said. 'Bugs are beautiful too.'

'If you make them beautiful,' I said stubbornly.

Sophia laughed. 'Yeah, yeah, fair point. I wouldn't usually wait for the sun to come out. You were right.'

Pleased, I glanced around the dingy alley. Something caught my eye: a crushed drinks can nestled in a patch of straggly grass, maybe ten metres away along the wall. There must have been something interesting inside it, because a particularly ugly crow flapped down to it, shot us a wary look, and then began to poke at it with its beak.

'Can I borrow your camera?' I ventured. 'It's much better than mine.'

I'd been dying to ask. I'd wondered why such a splendid and obviously expensive camera was covered in scratches and dents, and how anybody could be so careless as to chip the plastic at the corner of the lens. But now that I'd seen the war zones and disaster areas it had visited, I understood.

Sophia hesitated for a few moments, then handed it over. 'We're a team, aren't we?'

I was right – her telephoto lens was amazing. By the time I stood up I was thrilled with my pictures, even though I had to peer hard at the screen to see them. I'd caught the bird head-on. Most of the crow was out of focus, but its beak, one huge menacing eye, a couple of blades of grass and the top of the can were needle-sharp.

'How about that?' I showed the screen to Sophia.

'"Here's a crow"?' She grinned again. 'No, I'm

kidding. That's definitely not just "Here's a crow".'

'Thanks!' I was so happy, my voice was squeaky.

'Can I ask you something?'

'Sure.' I nodded, slightly nervous.

'Your mum photographs birds too, doesn't she? I mean, that's where you got it. I remember you telling the club once.'

I nodded again, enthusiastically. 'She's really good at it. She's had them published. I mean, it's not like your mum, but she's great at what she does. She loves birds.'

'Martin.' Sophia shut one eye. 'Martin, did she call you after a kind of bird?'

I went redder than I'd ever gone before in a conversation with Sophia, and that was saying something. My face felt hot.

'Uh,' I croaked. 'Yes. Yeah, she did.'

'I knew it! I knew it! I mean,' she added hurriedly,

'I just had a suspicion. Alisha didn't believe me.'

'Alisha?' I scowled. I had a sudden bad feeling, but then I often did when Alisha was mentioned.

Sophia seemed suddenly fascinated by the floor. I realized I wasn't the only one who could blush. So she wasn't always cool, then.

'Ah,' she said, glancing up at me at last, 'the truth is, we had a bit of a debate about it. I said to Alisha that I thought your mum had called you after a bird. Sorry.'

'Humph,' I grunted. They talked about me. I knew it.

'Oh, don't look so offended. It was only a bit of fun. I promise. Honest.'

'Yeah, all right.' I shrugged, and suddenly it did seem quite funny. 'I don't mind, but I do get really annoyed when my mum actually tells people that's what she did.'

Sophia gave a hoot of laughter. 'OK, I get that. You do have your own parent problems, don't you?'

I couldn't help laughing too. 'Tell me about it!'

'So anyway, I reckon I can stay out another hour.' She zipped her camera into its bag, her face cheerful. 'What time is your dad picking you up?'

'Teatime,' I said, glancing at my watch.

'Great!' She gave me a mischievous grin. 'Because I know where we can find some really attractive cockroaches.'

* * *

'That,' I said as we walked away from the cafe at the end of Sophia's street, 'is the last time I buy a sandwich in there.'

'Oh come on,' Sophia nudged me. 'They're only around the outside drain. Oh, and under the porch, in the leaf litter. I'm sure there aren't any in the actual cafe.'

'And they were very photogenic,' I grinned.

'See? Now you're getting the idea.' She actually giggled, which was such an unusual sound from Sophia, it made me laugh.

'Hey! You found her! Hey Sophia, hey Marty! What's so funny?'

I knew that voice. My heart sank as Alisha and her friends hurried towards us.

'Hi, Alisha.' Sophia sounded slightly wary.

Maybe she was embarrassed to be seen with me. 'Nothing.'

'So he wasn't kidding? You two really are going to be a team?' Daisy's eyes were wide.

'Yes,' I said quickly, before Sophia could get a chance to disown me.

She shot me an odd look. 'Yes, Daisy. We're doing Miss Bartlett's competition.'

'Well, that's ... different,' muttered Maryam.

'That's kind of the point,' said Sophia sharply. 'We're different. Should be interesting.'

'Oh.' Alisha looked taken aback. 'I suppose you do have that photography stuff in common.'

'Yes,' said Sophia. 'We do.'

'So how's it going?' Alisha seemed less sure of herself now, but there was still a touch of challenge in her voice. 'Is Marty getting you to take lots of bird pictures? Isn't that his thing? I remember you said that.'

I squirmed inwardly. I could just imagine the things Sophia had said about my 'Here's an owl' picture.

Sophia glanced at me, then back at Alisha. 'Yep. Martin's giving me loads of tips.'

'Marty's giving you tips!' Alisha laughed. Then she seemed to realize, at the same time I did, that Sophia wasn't laughing.

'Uh-huh. He's actually really good,' said Sophia, staring hard at Alisha.

'Oh.' Alisha shrugged. For a moment she seemed lost for words. 'That's not what you ... I mean, last week, you ... ' She hesitated. 'Well, I suppose if that's how you want to spend a Sunday afternoon.'

'I do! It's great.' Sophia's eyes glinted. 'You should try it some time. Hey, Daisy, it beats gossiping on the swings in the park all day.'

Daisy went red, and her lips were tight. 'Oh,' was all she could say.

'Well, see you guys later.' Sophia gave them a brilliant smile, then pulled me past them and walked briskly away. I barely had time to give the three of them an awkward wave goodbye. I just caught Maryam's indignant voice – 'But she always says she's too busy to hang out with us, Alisha!' – and then we were out of earshot.

Sophia walked on in silence for a while, and I didn't dare say a word. At last she said, 'Sorry about that.'

'What?' I asked, though I thought I knew.

'Look, don't take it personally. Alisha's nice, you know? We just joke around sometimes.'

I had never imagined Sophia could sound so mortified. But then, I'd never imagined her defending me to Alisha, either.

'It's fine,' I said. And I realized it really was.

Chapter 7
Time Management

'I like these. I really do.' Mrs Sanders was gazing at her laptop as Sophia scrolled through the pictures we'd taken.

'You do?' Sophia eyed her sideways. She was kneeling beside the armchair, tilting the laptop screen now and again to make sure her mum could see the photos clearly.

'I do. I mean it.' Mrs Sanders glanced down at her and smiled. 'Martin's been a good influence!'

I felt ridiculously pleased at the compliment, though I did catch the wry look Sophia shot me. I could almost hear her thinking, *Wait, I've been a good influence on him too ...*

'You make a good team,' said Mrs Sanders. 'I had a feeling you would.' She leaned forward awkwardly, winced and sighed in frustration, then picked up her handy-grabber, rather as if she hated it. Trying again, she used the grabber to tap the photo Sophia loved, the one of the woman cooking in the rubble. 'Don't get me wrong, Sophia, I loved your photos before. But remember what I told you about finding the light among the dark?'

Sophia angled her face towards me and secretly rolled her eyes. 'Yeah, yeah.'

'If you have a spark of light, you can actually see the darkness better. And the other way round, too.'

'Yeah, yeah.'

'Yeah, yeah,' her mum mimicked her fondly. 'Honestly, Martin, I did try to tell her. But who listens to their mum?' She winked. 'Maybe it had to be you. Sophia doesn't listen to me about anything.'

'Oh, come on,' protested Sophia, irritated.

'Well, it's true.' Mrs Sanders tapped the grabber gently on her daughter's head. 'I told you yesterday you didn't need to be back so soon. I could have got to the fridge perfectly well and heated up some soup.'

The look Sophia gave her was a little stern.

'Or if I didn't,' her mum went on, 'it wouldn't have killed me to wait another hour. You don't have to dance attendance on me, Sophes. You could see your friends a bit more at the weekends.'

'Well, we got plenty of photos taken, so it worked out fine.' Sophia stood up with the laptop in her arms. 'Anyway, you look like you could use a rest now.'

'I'm fine. I can look at these some more ... '

Sophia took no notice. 'C'mon, Martin, we'll go to the kitchen and I'll get you a drink.'

I followed her through; Mrs Sanders's eyes were already closed. Maybe Sophia did know better than her mother. Sometimes.

Sophia set down the laptop on the kitchen table and opened the fridge. She withdrew a couple of juice cartons and stuck a straw in each, then sat down and glared at the laptop screen. She was getting her scary look back, I decided. Maybe because she looked tired today.

Her mum's carer isn't back till Monday, I remembered guiltily. *I guess Sophia had to cook for her last night, and get her to bed.* My Saturday night had been spent on the sofa, my legs hooked over the arm, watching a science fiction DVD with my parents.

'Your mum sounds like she can cope OK,' I ventured. 'When you're not here, I mean.'

'Don't you believe it,' snapped Sophia. She shrugged, eyes still fixed on the laptop. 'I mean, she used to have some good days. Like normal. But not many now.'

'Oh.' It was hard to know what to say. 'She seems to appreciate you, anyway. All the stuff you do.'

'Humph. Not always. She can be pretty bad-tempered. If she's frustrated. I don't know if you've noticed but she hates that ugly grabber-thing. She's angry about not being able to go upstairs and sit in her own study. And she blows a fuse if her hand shakes and she spills her tea.'

I felt sorry for Mrs Sanders and for Sophia, but at the same time oddly pleased that she would be this open with me. And I certainly wasn't going to let on about feeling sorry for her; she'd probably kick me. 'You said she's got carers?'

'Yeah, but they're not here all the time, are they? And I know her best.' She said the last part rather proudly. 'By the way, she still works, you know. Sometimes. She writes for a photography magazine and she did an article in a Sunday paper last month, all about her work in Colombia. She's not helpless so don't go thinking she is!' She scowled. 'Though she did lose her temper last week when she went to reach for her stick and knocked her laptop off the table.'

I decided to stay quiet, since I kept saying the wrong thing.

'Anyway,' Sophia went on defensively, 'it's ridiculous that she worries about me. I'm fine. I'm not the one with MS.'

'What is … ? I mean, what does … ?'

'Her muscles don't get messages properly from her brain. Look.' Sophia bent the straw in her carton and sucked on it. 'Like that. I'm trying to drink, but the straw's broken so the juice can't get through. And I can straighten it out – see? – and that's fine for a while but now the straw's squished and it's got a kink and it'll keep getting worse. It'll get harder and harder to drink through it.' She tossed the straw aside and got herself a new one. 'So she won't get better, but she's not dying or anything.'

Oh. Thank goodness. I tried to look as if I hadn't wanted to ask.

'But she won't get better,' said Sophia again, sadly. 'But she's still really good at the stuff she can do. I'll let you see her articles. They're great.'

She was being confusing again and I wasn't sure what to say. Because I was stuck, I actually started to say, 'I'm sorry ... '

'Yes, well, that's life. Enough about that.' She was brisk again. 'Let's talk about printing the photos out. We'll have to pick the best ones and make captions. And by the way, I've got a great idea for our team name ... '

Chapter 8
The Big Day

When I woke up two Fridays later, it was a few moments before I realized what the queasy feeling in my stomach was about. Then I blinked a few times, and it kicked in: it was competition day. I swallowed hard. I was very tempted to pull the duvet back over my head and pretend I was sick.

I had spent so much time and energy agreeing with Sophia that we were going to win, I hadn't stopped to think about whether we actually could.

Callie Smith was brilliant at photographing sunsets, for a start, and she'd teamed up with Haseena, who lived in a house overlooking the beach. I could imagine how amazing their entry was going to be. And then there were Ace and Daniel, who won a lot of competitions in all

kinds of subjects, because they were just so funny the teachers couldn't help liking them (when they weren't yelling at them).

My stomach dipped again. It was bad enough that I might not win, but I realized I cared more about Sophia's reaction. She'd been so cheerful the last few days, and I hadn't even let her think about losing. I hoped I wasn't going to let her down.

I gulped as my stomach dipped again.

Actually I might be coming down with something, I thought. *I'm sure I've got a temperature.*

'Mar-tin!' My mum's usual sing-song command drifted from the kitchen. 'Marrr-tiiin! Time to get up!'

I gritted my teeth and blinked my eyes clear. This was silly. Of course I wasn't ill, and I couldn't just not show up. That would really be letting Sophia down.

Somehow I managed to eat some cereal, though it tasted like dust and grit mixed with milk. Mum hustled me out of the house and we set off with Dad's 'Good luck, Martin!' ringing hollow in my ears. I trudged to school so slowly – despite Mum's cajoling and exasperated warnings – I almost ended up being late.

'Martin, you've got less than a minute!' she told me at last with a glance at her watch. 'Go on! It'll be fine. Your photos are wonderful. Good luck!' She was right about one thing; I could hear the bell. I gasped a panicked goodbye and had to run the last hundred metres.

I tore off my anorak and flung it at my hook; it missed, but I didn't have time to pick it up. I didn't even have time to look around the class; I just ran to my chair and slumped into it as Mr Gray started to read the day's announcements. There was something about a visit to the Breakness fire station next Thursday, and remembering to bring in stuff for the Spring Fayre.

' … And of course, this afternoon it's the judging for the Art Club photography competition.' He lifted his head and smiled at me, then at Ace and Daniel and some of the others. 'There are a few members of this class involved, so we're all looking forward to seeing your work. Miss Bartlett says it's been very hard to choose the winners, and she won't tell me who they are.' He scowled jokingly. 'But good luck, all of you!'

I turned to catch Sophia's eye, and that was when I realized.

She wasn't there.

* * *

Break time seemed to take an age to arrive. I couldn't concentrate on a single word of our class reading book, and even the fun science experiment felt like an endless chore. As soon as the bell buzzed, I darted out to hunt for Alisha in the corridor, but she found me first.

'Hey, Marty!' She hurried up to me, her face creased in a frown of worry. She took my arm and bustled me out into the playground. 'What's with Sophia? Why isn't she here?'

'I was just going to ask you that.' I shrugged helplessly. It wasn't possible to be scared of Alisha when she looked so nervous herself.

'She only stays off school when her mum really needs her.' Alisha chewed her nails. 'But I saw both of them yesterday and Mrs Sanders was OK.'

'Maybe ... ' I said, and swallowed guiltily, because I'd nearly called in sick myself. 'Maybe she's too nervous about the competition?'

'Oh, I don't think so.' Alisha shook her head, but she didn't look certain. 'Seriously? Do you think? But she was looking forward to it, Marty. She was really excited.'

'She was?' I asked, though I'd got that feeling too.

'Yes, she was. Actually,' she said, and studied me with narrowed eyes, 'I think she's enjoyed the whole thing. Working with you, I mean.'

I blinked.

Alisha shuffled uncomfortably and folded her arms. 'I still think it's the nerdiest thing in the world, but she loves that camera of her mum's. And I don't think she'd have entered the competition at all if she hadn't teamed up with you.'

'Oh!' I was surprised, but pleased.

'But,' added Alisha firmly, 'that makes it even

weirder that she isn't here. I really hope her mum's all right.'

'Do you think the school will let us phone her?'

'I doubt it.' Alisha shrugged. 'But maybe if you ask Miss Bartlett … '

That was an idea. I was pretty sure Miss Bartlett would be nearly as disappointed as I was that Sophia hadn't turned up. And if it was nervousness keeping her away, a teacher was much more likely than I was to persuade her to come in after all. I hoped there wasn't anything seriously wrong at Sophia's, of course, but the truth was I did *not* want to go to the competition judging on my own.

'OK, I'll ask Miss Bartlett,' I said. 'Maybe she can phone.'

Alisha turned on her heel and began to walk away, then turned back to glare a warning at me. 'Don't let me down, Marty.'

Alisha, believe me. Never mind Sophia and the competition. I am way too scared of you to let you down.

Chapter 9
Emergency!

'I'm sorry, Miss Bartlett, I know you were busy organizing the prize-giving this lunchtime ... '

'Never mind that!' she told me briskly, peering over the steering wheel and making the turn into Broxden Street. 'It's much more important to find out if Sophia's OK. She called in this morning to say she had to stay with her mum, but if she's having problems there really should be emergency care cover. I'll see what I can do.'

'Thanks for letting me come,' I mumbled. I'd begged her, after all.

'That's all right, Martin.' She spared me a quick smile. 'I've got your consent form that says you can come out with me on Art Club projects. And I think this counts as an Art Club project! Quick, you go in while I park properly.'

As I ran up the ramp to Sophia's front door, I realized we had twenty minutes before the school bell rang. Make that half an hour, because the whole school was going straight to the dining hall for the competition announcement, and everyone would be milling around for a while. There would be a fair amount of chaos for ten minutes or so, which gave me a bit of extra time. But I didn't want to miss the prize announcements ...

I was thinking so hard about that, I didn't realize I was leaning on the doorbell.

'What?' The door was flung open, and Sophia glared at me. Her eyes widened, and she blinked. 'Martin! What are you doing here?'

'Never mind that,' I gasped, still out of breath. 'What are *you* doing *here*?'

'I ... ' For once, she looked lost for words.

'It's competition day!' I said.

She looked defiant. 'I couldn't get to school today. My mum's not well. Sorry.'

'Sophia?' a voice called from inside the house. 'Is that Martin I hear?'

Sophia set her jaw. 'Yes, Mum,' she called over her shoulder. 'He's just popped in. He's got to get back to school.'

'Doesn't he have time to say hello?'

For a long moment, Sophia locked eyes with me.

'Miss Bartlett's here,' I said, unnecessarily, as she appeared at my back at that exact moment.

'Hello, Sophia.' Miss Bartlett gave her a concerned smile. 'We wanted to make sure you're all right. Martin and I both knew you wouldn't want to miss the judging unless it was an emergency. Is everything OK?'

Sophia dropped her stare at last, stepped back and let us come in.

Nervously I edged past her. 'We'll just say hello,' I whispered guiltily. 'Really quickly.'

Sophia glanced at her watch and opened the living room door.

Mrs Sanders does look tired today, I thought. She was drawn and pale, and she was rubbing her knee awkwardly with her wrist, but she smiled at me.

'Hello, Martin. Miss Bartlett, how nice to see you!' She looked a little taken aback.

'Lovely to see you, too, Mrs Sanders,' enthused Miss Bartlett. 'I do hope you're feeling better?'

'Hi, Mrs Sanders.' That was me out of things to say. Sophia was standing behind me, arms folded.

Her mum creased her brow. 'Um ... I'm pleased to see you both, but this is a little ... unexpected.'

'Well, yes, but ... we just wanted to see if Sophia was OK ... ' I chewed my lip. 'Because it's competition day and everything, I guessed you might not be well and—'

'It's competition day!' Her eyes flew open. 'Oh Miss Bartlett, I'm so sorry! Sophia, you didn't remind me! Off you go!'

'Don't be daft, Mum,' growled Sophia. 'You're poorly today.'

'I wasn't very well this morning,' said Mrs Sanders. 'I'm feeling better now and Denise is coming in later. The lady from the carers,' she explained, with a glance at me and Miss Bartlett. 'I'll be fine, Sophia.'

'No, you won't. You were really tired and you had a lot of pain.'

'I *was* and I *had*. I told you, I feel much better. You must go to school, Sophia. You've put such a lot of work into this!'

'This is more important!' Sophia sounded as if she might be about to cry.

'You're important too!' Mrs Sanders had raised her voice, and she sounded severe. 'You absolutely don't have to stay, Sophia. You can ask the school if you can phone me later, just to check. I'm sure Miss Bartlett can arrange that?' She glanced at the teacher, who nodded eagerly. 'But Denise will be here in an hour.'

'I can't go!' blurted Sophia furiously.

'Yes, I'm telling you,' her mum told her with irritation. 'You can – oh. Oh, I see!' She blinked at Sophia. 'Sweetheart, you don't have to be nervous about the competition.'

Sophia folded her arms again. She scowled at the floor. She sighed.

'Maybe I don't have to be,' she said at last. 'But I still am.'

'What?' I blinked. 'But you're the one who told me it would be fine!'

'Yeah, well, I'm not sure now!' she snapped.

I fidgeted with the sleeve of my jumper. Miss Bartlett was giving nothing away; it had been driving me crazy all morning. I'd had not so much as a smile or a wink from her. When she wanted to be stony-faced and secretive, she was really surprisingly good at it.

'We don't have to win,' I muttered.

'You said we did!' With an embarrassed glance at Miss Bartlett, Sophia grunted, 'I mean, so did I, I know that, but now that it's here ... '

'I know,' I mumbled. 'It is kind of scary. But winning doesn't matter. Honest. Look, I just want you to be there when they show the photos. They're good. It'll be a shame if you're not there after all your hard work.'

'I absolutely agree,' put in Miss Bartlett, who seemed to be letting me do most of the talking.

It made me downright depressed that she was giving not the slightest hint about the winners; it wasn't a good sign. When I'd handed in our project at the start of the week, Miss Bartlett had looked a bit surprised, as if it wasn't what she'd expected. She hadn't said a word, so I had a very bad feeling about our chances.

'Martin and Miss Bartlett are right,' Mrs Sanders said firmly. 'I think you're both in with a good chance, but Sophes – that's not the point.' She reached out a shaky hand, and Sophia took it a little reluctantly. 'I've loved watching you do this, the last couple of weeks. You've been so excited, and so into it, and you've been bursting with ideas. You've been thinking about something other than me.'

'I think about other things all the time!' Sophia objected.

'Not nearly enough! You need to have fun and just be a young girl. That's what makes me feel better, OK?'

I saw Sophia squeeze her mum's hand a little.
'But it'll be so embarrassing if we lose.'

'I don't care if that happens,' I told her.
'That's not true,' Sophia mocked me.

'I'm not listening to this, by the way,' put in Miss Bartlett seriously. 'The judges have made their decisions already, but Sophia, listen – Martin and your mum are right. You deserve to be there just for all the work you've put in.'

I cleared my throat nervously. 'The thing is, Sophia, I've had fun too. It's been brilliant doing this with you, and I even enjoyed looking for the cockroaches.' I grinned. 'It's worth it even if we come last.'

For the first time, I saw the twitch of a smile at the corner of Sophia's mouth. Then she pursed her lips and glowered at me, but her eyes were sparkling.

'No way are we coming last.' She shot a challenging grin at Miss Bartlett. 'All right, it's a deal. If you're sure you're OK, Mum?'

'Sophia, for goodness' sake, I am one hundred per cent *positive*.'

'Right, Martin. Let's go!'

Chapter 10
Team Players

When she parked beside the playground, Miss Bartlett dashed off with barely a word of goodbye. Sophia and I missed the bell, but only by seconds; as I'd hoped, pupils were still filing into the hall (well, squeezing eagerly through a bottleneck at the swing doors while the teachers called out directions), and Sophia and I joined the back of the bustling queue. We exchanged a glance of relief, and Sophia tugged her collar away from her throat and whispered, *'Phew!'*

'We made it,' I said, rubbing my face.

'Let's see if we're getting a consolation prize,' murmured Sophia, but there was a hint of cheerful optimism in her voice.

'Can you see our display?' I asked anxiously. Two of the walls were covered in the big sheets of coloured card Miss Bartlett had told us to use; even from here I could make out a few of the photos on them, and some were amazing. Lots of the displays had beautiful lettering and imaginatively decorated borders. There were at least twenty entries altogether; the competition had been more popular than I'd realized. My heart sank again.

'There.' Sophia pointed at a corner of the room. 'There's ours!'

It was sandwiched between two displays of animals: one of various farm creatures, and one of an assortment of exotic monkeys from the nearest zoo. The nearest zoo was miles away.

'Somebody got a weekend trip from their parents,' whispered Sophia, with a tinge of envy.

'It doesn't matter,' I reassured her. 'We had the most fun, right?'

'Right.'

I hesitated. 'Are you still glad you came?'

I thought she wasn't going to answer, but: 'Yeah.' She nodded slowly. 'Yes, I am. Thanks, Martin.'

I couldn't help smiling. Whatever happened, I was glad I'd persuaded her to come. But we couldn't talk any more, because we'd all sat down on the floor now, and Miss Bartlett was raising a hand.

The hubbub died away as everyone raised their hands in response.

'Good afternoon, boys and girls. The waiting is over!' Miss Bartlett sounded as if she was introducing the final of a television talent show. 'Welcome to the results of the Art Club Photography Competition! Now, first I'm going to introduce you to my fellow judges: Mr Knox, the editor of the *Breakness Gazette*, is our local celebrity! We also have our own head teacher and school celebrity – Mrs Brownlee!'

There was a burst of over-enthusiastic clapping, led by Mr Gray; everyone had actually been wound up to quite a pitch of excitement. I suddenly felt sick again, and I couldn't concentrate on what Miss Bartlett was saying. It wasn't anything vital: some stuff about how difficult the judging had been with so many marvellous entries; a bit about the *Breakness Gazette*; some gushing thank-yous to local companies for the prize donations. It was getting hot in the hall. Outside, sunlight had broken through the clouds, and there was a patch of it streaming in through the windows and baking me. I thought I was going to melt, or maybe faint.

Now that would be embarrassing. I shook myself and pulled off my jumper.

'And now we come to the moment of truth!' Miss Bartlett clapped her hands, eyes shining. 'I wish I had time to show you all the entries properly, but I'm going to tell you something about the top three before we announce the winner.'

Oh no. This was torture. I heard Sophia give a muffled groan.

'I've photographed and enlarged all the boards and put them on a slideshow so we can all see them properly.' Miss Bartlett clicked on a laptop mouse. 'Can we close the curtains, Mr Gray?'

Well, that's something. I blew out a sigh of relief as Mr Gray shut out the blazing sun.

'Now,' said Miss Bartlett, as a slide appeared on the screen behind her. 'This is such a good example of what I was looking for.' She gestured grandly at the display of photos, all neatly captioned. 'This is from Team Mermaid! Take a bow, girls!'

Haseena and Callie got to their feet, shuffling and giggling at the sudden attention as we all applauded.

'They've used disposable waterproof cameras to give us two very different views of the sea,' said Miss Bartlett. 'These beautiful sunsets from the beach – and here are the same sunsets from just below the water's surface. Look at the light! Look how it changes on top of the water and under the water! And the way you've set out your photographs is like even more reflections. Well done, girls!'

'Why didn't we think of that?' Sophia looked miserable. 'That's brilliant.'

'They probably got their shoes wet,' I whispered consolingly.

'Now.' Miss Bartlett clicked the mouse. 'We also loved this collage of monkeys from Sandwood Zoo.'

'I knew it,' groaned Sophia under her breath.

'But it's not just the really excellent photographs, of course. All the judges were very impressed with how much thought went into this, from the team called Going Bananas. Stand up, you two!'

I recognized the two kids who got to their feet: Zara and Calum from Year 5. They were trying to look solemn but they were obviously thrilled to bits, and kept breaking into smiles.

'We all loved how you took photos of people, too, doing the same sort of thing as the monkeys. The people in the cafe eating crisps and the toddler swinging on the monkey bars. That's your sister, is it Zara? Anyway, very clever observations, congratulations!'

Miss Bartlett was murmuring to the other judges,

shuffling bits of paper. She raised her head and beamed at us again.

'Oh, I almost forgot! The judges want to give a special mention to this display: "How We USUALLY See The World", by Aces High!'

She clicked again, and up came a chaotic collage of photographs. Half of them were upside down, as if the photographer had been hanging off a climbing frame. (And I'm sure he had been.) One of the pictures was just a wild blur of grass, and it was obvious he'd fallen off as he was taking it. Another picture showed a familiar muddy trainer, stuck skywards, and another was a sideways view of an angry looking squirrel.

'There aren't any captions on these,' she said, wagging a finger mock-severely. 'But as the title says it all, I think we can overlook that.' Miss Bartlett laughed. 'And I'm sure we can all guess which team's worldview this is. Take a bow, Ace and Daniel!'

They sprang to their feet, grinning and high-fiving one another. Ace tumbled over into a handstand and Daniel grabbed his legs to steady him – which was probably how they'd taken most of their photos.

I couldn't help laughing, even though the disappointment was sharp. Sophia was smiling ruefully, too, as she clapped. 'I guess the monkeys are going to win,' she murmured, and added with a grin, 'the real ones, I mean. It was worth a try, though. I had fun, Martin.'

'Me too. I'm sorry we—'

'Hush now,' said Miss Bartlett loudly, quietening the room. 'Back to the top three!'

'Oh.' Sophia looked more shocked than relieved, as if she couldn't bear any more tension. I knew how she felt. I was hearing that shutter-click in my heart again.

'It was a tough decision – so close – but we've awarded third prize to Going Bananas, and the runners-up are Team Mermaid. So now we come to the winning team, and I can now reveal they are ... '

Miss Bartlett took a dramatic breath.

'Team Sandmartin!'

I thought the disappointment had finally been too much for Sophia, because she gave a high-pitched scream.

Then I realized she was jumping to her feet and

dragging me along with her – which was when
I remembered her great idea for a team name.

'Well done, Sophia and Martin!' Miss Bartlett was
grinning from ear to ear as she clicked on her mouse
and up came a slide of our display.

I couldn't move, since I could hardly breathe,
but Sophia was making up for it anyway. She was
bouncing up and down, and she turned and gave me
a sudden hug.

'All the judges felt this was a stand-out winner,'
Miss Bartlett went on. 'The images are so beautiful,
and so technically brilliant. I told the Art Club all
about light and dark, and this team have really taken
that to heart. Look at this cockroach, struggling up
out of the leaves.' She smiled at us, then turned back
to the screen.

'I don't think any of you have ever thought of a bug as brave and beautiful before! Team Sandmartin calls this one "Reaching for the Sky".' (There were a few cries of *'Ewwww! Yuck!'* from the younger classes at this point, but mostly the audience just listened attentively.)

'And here are two wonderful photos that look very similar, but one's of a seagull and the other is a bit of old rubbish. What is it, Martin, a supermarket bag? Yes, we thought so! They've called this one "Here's a Seagull", which is funny, you see, because they've put that caption under the bag, not the bird.'

She went on explaining our artwork for longer, but I honestly didn't hear any more – partly because I was too thrilled and excited to concentrate, and partly because of the whoops and cheers from the audience.

Mr Gray shot us a wink and a smile. 'Excellent teaching, you see,' he said quite loudly, and we both giggled.

Alisha's voice was even louder than his, though. 'Yay, Sophia! Yay, Marty!' she yelled. She gave me a grin that wasn't mocking at all, and I realized she was genuinely pleased.

'Yay for the camera nerds!'

* * *

I clutched my new digital pocket camera very tightly, determined not to drop it as I hunted for Sophia. I'd lost sight of her in the crowd after the competition announcement, and even Alisha didn't know where she'd gone. But I finally spotted her coming out of the school secretary's office. She was still beaming broadly, as if the smile would never leave her face.

I realized straight away what she'd been doing. 'Is your mum OK?'

'She's fine. Mrs Brownlee said I could phone her. And Mum says congratulations to you too, by the way! She knew you were a brilliant photographer.'

'Wow.' I blushed. Mrs Sanders really said that? It was almost better than my new pocket digital camera. 'You are too, of course.'

'Thanks, Martin.' Her grin grew even broader. 'I am so happy!'

I felt suddenly awkward. I stuck out a hand, not knowing what else to do. 'Well, thanks for being my partner. It really was fun.'

'Oh,' she said, her smile fading a little as she solemnly shook my hand. 'I guess that's the competition finished now. It worked great in the end. I'm glad you talked me into it.'

'I loved the way our display looked. Oh, and the team name! That was great. I'd completely forgotten it. I didn't know who Miss Bartlett was talking about.'

Sophia beamed. 'I was pleased with it. It's a kind of bird, you know. I looked it up online.'

'I, uh … I know.'

She laughed, and I realized she'd been teasing. 'Yeah, anyway, it's such a good name it seems a shame to drop it, doesn't it?'

'Huh?' I tilted my head. 'How do you mean?'

Sophia nibbled at her lip and glanced away awkwardly. 'Well, I know I made a fuss about the whole team thing to start with. But I did enjoy it. Turned out it was pretty smart of Miss Bartlett to put us together.'

'Uh-huh.' I narrowed my eyes thoughtfully. 'Sometimes I wonder if she did it deliberately.'

'And, anyway, I thought we could maybe do some more photography projects, you know. Together.'

I could not hold back my broad grin. 'I was kind of hoping you'd say that.'

'Great!' Sophia laughed. 'We can talk about it properly at next week's Art Club. Meanwhile ... ' She shrugged casually. 'Mum's having some friends round tonight for pizza and a movie. She was wondering if you'd like to come? And your parents? They can hang out with the grown-ups. My mum's really keen to meet your mum so she can jabber on about photography. Her words.'

I laughed. 'Yeah, we'd love to!'

'You're on, then. I'd really like that too.' She smiled. 'And so would Mum. You're such a hit with her.'

We walked out of the school doors together, raving about our new cameras as we tore them out of the packaging. Miss Bartlett was opening her car door as we passed, and she glanced up with a smile.

'Thanks for the cameras, Miss B,' called Sophia.

'You deserved them!' she called back cheerfully. 'Great work, you two. You made a good team!'

She smiled and waved. And I definitely heard her add, in a not-quite-quiet-enough chuckle:

'I always knew you would.'